Control is *Not* a Four-Letter Word!

Control is *Not* a Four-Letter Word!

Establishing Positive Classroom Behavior
for the Year in the First Five Days

Sarah Clancy-Ballard

INFORMATION AGE PUBLISHING, INC.
Charlotte, NC • www.infoagepub.com

Library of Congress Cataloging-in-Publication Data

A CIP record for this book is available from the Library of Congress
http://www.loc.gov

ISBN: 978-1-68123-926-2 (Paperback)
      978-1-68123-927-9 (Hardcover)
      978-1-68123-928-6 (ebook)

Printed in the United States of America

Dedication

I stand on the shoulders of my family, constantly steadied by the hand and heart of my husband of half a century, encouraged by our incredible three children, and immeasurably enriched by our ten grandchildren.

I am also indebted to my dear, dear sister-in-law, Eve Ballard, who has been a driving force behind this endeavor and incredibly generous with her time and suggestions not only in graphic design, but also in all aspects of this publication. In addition, I must recognize a friend, Ellie Blair, who brings me not only encouragement, but extraordinary editing skill and professional expertise in the publication world.

This book is dedicated to them and to my aunt, Elizabeth Ruth Wilson, my precious gadfly, who never allowed me (and many others) to settle for "less" when "more" was possible.

Always she asked, "How are you giving back to your community?"

Contents

Introduction

I N THE BEGINNING...

The beginning was when I walked into a fourth grade classroom in 1966—shortly after, I was hired to teach. I might have been prepared for many things that hot August morning, but teaching a classroom of diverse little creatures, each somebody's darling (or should have been), I was not prepared. I was hired on a Friday. A teacher had resigned during preplanning, and I started on a Monday, with a provisional certificate. My classroom was part of the original educational facility built in the 1940s and was comprised of three rooms, a small hall and a storage closet. Due to population increase, the newer building had filled and this little building of three rooms was pressed back into service. I thanked God daily for the two veteran teachers who were on either side of my room. It was only through their kindness and expertise that I made it through that first year without having a nervous breakdown. However, on some days, it seemed like a breakdown might be preferable to another day of school.

I quickly realized the most important things I learned, while attending Converse College, were how to improvise (Thank you, Mr. Parker, Acting 101); how to speak correctly and communicate with a group of children (Ms. Sherman, Public Speaking and Children's Theatre) and how to organize (Mr. Nesbit, Directing 201, 202). I mention these courses for all of you who do not realize that whatever your training, up to this point, some of the relative areas of learning may come from a class that does not have EDU attached to it. Be *open* and *creative* and stay that way.

Some of you may be new college graduates who decided to go into a state or federal program that rewards you for taking positions in places where there are almost no certified teachers. It waives certification requirements, pays very little, and may help reduce your student loans. It sounds like a wonderful way to enlist the brains, enthusiasm, and altruistic hearts of young people and give them a chance to get the experience all employers expect you to have. (I still have not figured that one out!) However, many will get through this experience because of energy and good teaching intuition. If you are in this group, I wish you well and tell you that preparation and control are going to be even *more* imperative in this scenario because you are probably going to be fraught with economic and social issues that a veteran teacher would find daunting. I applaud the programs that are reaching into such needy areas. I am deeply saddened by the knowledge that so many of our children are not being reached.

There has long been discussion as to the relevance and/or helpfulness the EDU classes provide. While I believe the origin of this bias lies in the fact that much of the EDU content may not provide the immediate assistance the novice instructor needs. Until actually in the classroom, it may be difficult for the beginning teacher to recognize the application of knowledge learned in the college and university educational classes. Additionally, I believe there are some classic misconceptions about students and the student-teacher relationship . . . going as far back as the troublemakers in *Little House on the Prairie*, or in *21 Jump Street, Saved by the Bell, My So Called Life, Boston Public*, et al.!

It is the goal of this manual to provide a bridge between the college classroom, where you were the *student*, and to your classroom now where you are the *teacher*. For all of you who have always wanted to teach and gone through the teacher preparation program, and/or are simply a natural born teacher (there are a few) and love your job, congratulations! You are doing the most important job in society, except parenting. I wish you years of satisfaction and success.

At any rate, there I was in the middle of a dusty, non-air conditioned room, wood walls, and floors. (Did I mention this was in Georgia where it only gets cool ten minutes every other day in January and February?) One sidewall permitted the door to the hall and some built in cubbies for books with a low table and three little chairs pushed up to the corner. Across the front wall stretched one long, very dusty chalkboard. Three large windows intersected the other wall providing the room's only ventilation and an open invitation to any insect interested in our activities. The coat hooks across the back wall remained empty the majority of the school year.

The twenty-five desks were in three long rows facing the board. The teacher desk was at the front, facing the children. Looking around the room, I became aware of the fact that I was *not* prepared! I most definitely was not in any way, shape or form, prepared. Another prayer quickly whispered, "Thank you, God, that I have my Irish ancestor's good humor and ability to face life's unexpected blessings which frequently come in the form of disaster. Amen."

Forty years later, I know beyond a shadow of a doubt and in spite of the advice of many textbooks which offer endless lofty solutions to classroom management and academic success, that the bottom line for teacher and student success is preparation (teacher *and* student) and teacher control. The levels of preparedness, which both bring to the classroom, and the depth of commitment the teacher has to control of the class, are key. Now well into my third year of retirement, I still dream of the classroom, at least weekly. Most dreams end in a dilemma resulting from a lack of preparation. Fear of not being prepared is definitely a teacher related neurosis that comes with the territory. With such angst still reverberating in my subconscious I feel compelled to put pen to paper, or finger to keyboard, as the times require, and "share."

How to Use This Manual

I hope that the information is presented in a clear and logical way. Some people learn best by reading cover to cover. Others fare better by skimming areas of interest as listed under *Contents* that catch their eye. There are a few of you out there who like to sneak a peek at the back to see if there is a sure fire shortcut to *the* answer. (Frankly, that is the type of learner/reader I am and I really understand you.) However, sadly there is *not* just *one*, heaven-sent, miraculous answer. Sorry.

I have kept this text short, but interactive because teachers (or almost teachers) are generally smart, motivated and do not have one extra minute to spend on talking something to death . . . I have tried to avoid the statement, restatement and the elaborated statement. I think it will be worth your time to think and jot down thoughts in the boxes that encourage you to reflect. It will sensitize you to the experience at hand, both yours and the students.

Reading through the whole thing should give you the BIG picture. Referring to specific needs should be easy enough with the table of contents and specific page numbers noted in parenthesis.

Feel free to highlight, an addiction I developed as a teacher, though I still feel a tad guilty "defacing" the written word. Underlining, turning corners of pages or anything else that helps you become "one" with the book is totally encouraged. Unfortunately, sleeping with it under your pillow at

Control Is Not a Four-Letter Word, pages xv–xvi
Copyright © 2017 by Information Age Publishing

night will definitely not help. (I tried that a few times as an undergraduate. To no avail.)

I hope that you will let three mantras echo in your head awake and asleep:

> Control is *not* a four-letter word.
> You must be in control of your class.
> Classroom control comes with *preparation*.

Dia dhuit! (God be with you)

Education is the most powerful weapon, which you can use to change the world.

—Nelson Mandela

PART 1

First Impressions

We all live under the same sky, but we all do not have the same horizon.

—Konrad Adenauer

1

First Impressions

Learning takes place in an environment
of trust.

Your Appearance

The expression on your face is paramount. It immediately sets the tone. You should be standing at the door as your students come into the room. No excuses. No "chatting it up" with the teacher next door. No hiding behind the desk, sitting on it, or leaning against it. Stand straight and look the student in the eye. So, while standing at the door with a seating chart in your hand, greet each personally. Be familiar with the chart.

Say your name clearly. Ask them their name and repeat it in a sentence, such as, "Tom, glad to meet you. (You might add a personal remark, such as "I saw you earlier in the hall.") "Your seat, Tom, is _____." (There is a theory that if you repeat the name of a person you have just met three times, making sure to look at him or her each time before going on to another person or activity that you will remember their name. It does work.) What

Control Is NOT a Four Letter Word, pages 5–25
Copyright © 2017 by Information Age Publishing

we are really talking about is the student as an individual, and the fastest way for you to convey your sincere interest in him or her as an individual is by remembering his or her name. How does this relate to control? You will never be truly in charge of your class and effective in your instruction until each student feels you know them as an individual: the good, the bad, the ugly, and the beautiful diva. By the way, that knowledge may or may not make you especially fond of them. There is much about students, and their lives, with which you may have difficulty. The trick is to learn who they are and convey to them in a kind but professional manner your respect and regard for them.

YOUR CLASSROOM EXPERIENCES: *Recall some of your most memorable teachers.*

Favorite teacher:

Disliked teacher:

Reflections:

Getting Back to Your Face

It should not be a distraction. Recognizing that everyone is an individual, there is still room for the old cliché: There is a time and place for everything. Your personal choices regarding your appearance are valid, but in making those choices certain considerations need to be recognized. Excessive makeup, unkempt facial hair, and out of control hair of any kind will never work for you. Take a look around at the other teachers. You may be a cut above or below them. You decide. Just remember, when you look them straight in the eye, they will make a decision about you. They will decide if you like yourself, like your job, like them. Yes, that is what a face says.

Your Clothing

Clothing is also a component of the first impression. Although I am all about comfort on any given day and embrace the idea that I teach better when I am comfortable, it is not okay to wear the darling warm-up suit, even with sequins and rhinestones, or the school colored sports attire because you are a coach. I did, with gentle prodding and modeling from my favorite administrator, come around to the idea that one needs to look professional. That does not mean you have to be in a blue or black suit, but it does mean that your attire should be up-to-date in quality, clean, and neat. Personal taste always enters in your choice of clothing and no one wants to cramp your style. However, clothing needs to be attractive and functional. It is important that what you are wearing allows you freedom to do your job without distracting your students. This then rules out things that slip up or down when you reach to write on the board, lean over a desk, or squat down to retrieve something from the floor. Somewhere between the styles of Ma and Pa Kettle and Angelina and Brad, I am sure you can find clothing that clearly says to your students, "I'm here to teach."

YOUR THOUGHTS ABOUT PERSONAL APPEARANCE:

Your Speech

Then there is the speaking thing. I nearly went crazy in the last years of teaching because of the mumbling responses I heard from students, even when they did know the answer. Speech today is not what it was 30 years ago, among young or old. The lack of projection and articulation among people today is appalling, and if there is any hope that it will get better, it is in the classroom.

Effective and correct speaking in the classroom begins with you and the way you speak. Think about how effective a speaker you are. Do people always understand what you say? This may be a hard thing to determine from students in your classroom, since they may not be very discriminating listeners, but your peers might give you some input. Actually, I really think a speech class ought to be required of all students before graduating from high school and again in college. However, the real thing here is you. If you are not a good speaker, you need to be. Get your administrator to bring someone in to do a crash course at a faculty meeting. If you are still in school, sign up for a speech class. It is not rocket science; you can learn the fundamentals in an hour. However, it is about practicing correct speech and eliminating poor speech. Unfortunately, I have heard some extremely poor projection and articulation among faculty members, as well as a very mundane vocabulary. I may be stepping out a bit, but I believe educators should sound educated.

How does this relate to class control? Everything. Have you ever watched what happens to a group when a speaker drones through a lecture? It is total shutdown that is manifested in sleeping and other expressions of inattention, such as whispering, friendly notes, and text messaging. You need:

- Good volume
- Variety of pitch
- Tempo
- Animation of tone

And the animated face that says, "Listen up. This is great stuff I have to share with you."

Body Language

This is also extremely important. Frequently people unconsciously scream many negative things with their body. If you are having a bad day, you can bet your students will pick up on it quickly just by the way you walk, stand, lean, or sit. However, you do not need a class in body language. Become an observer for a day or two at school, at home, in the stores, wherever. Watch everybody you can (without getting labeled and locked up as a weirdo) and see how their bodies convey a myriad of emotions and attitudes. Think about how you possibly convey the same kind of negative things to the people (students) around you. Kids are sharp, and they are listening to what your body is saying. Be careful what you say. Be positive.

Greet your students at the door every day with a friendly face, calling them by name (not always easy to do).

YOUR THOUGHTS:

Classroom Appearance

Some may feel this does not apply to them because of the age of their students or their particular subject matter. If you think that you are completely wrong. We learn through all our senses.

The way your class:

- Looks
- Smells
- Is lit
- Sounds
- How desks are arranged
- How resources are placed
- Traffic pattern flows (or does not)

These are all factors that impact the learning that will or will not take place.

Cleanliness

The perception of these variables begins the moment the students enter the classroom.

You may or may not believe cleanliness is next to godliness, but it is for darn sure that an environment that smells or looks bad does not invite a positive response. That is the custodian's job, right? Yes, you are right, but if for whatever reason your room has not been cleaned, then you do it. Afterwards go to your administrator and find out how the situation can be remedied. You may be told to deal with it yourself because of any number of good or bad reasons. So what do you do then? Is it professional for you to clean? No. Is it professional to let your kids sit around in an unkempt and dirty room? No. Of course resigning is possible. Griping in the teachers' lounge is always an option. Fussing at the custodians might be considered. A letter to the board of education might get you some attention, possibly also putting you in your administrator's office for a little chat.

Go to the source—the kids. Aren't they creating the situation? Now young kids love to clean anything, anywhere (as long as it is not their house or own room) so you can make it their "reward" to be allowed to do a singular little thing, which when rewarding the appropriate number of kids, cleanup is accomplished in a snap. As students get older, the cleaning interest wanes. Fortunately, their messiness should also be on the wane. By middle and high school, you have to make it one of the "things we do—for the community."

Visual Stimulation

Getting them to buy into a sense of joint ownership of their environment is actually a very good thing, and your administrator will not have to have the "chat" with you about being a disgruntled employee. Even in my last years of teaching when a bit of the zealot had faded, I cleaned a carpet and even mopped a floor. I never thought I should do it, but there was no way that I was going to let my students sit in that environment. They were not getting the message from me that I didn't care. Believe me, the minute they think you don't care, it is all over. The students most assuredly will not care either, and thus the domino effect kicks in.

YOUR THOUGHTS:

Another thing you can do in the class appearance department is get real creative. Visual stimulus can help sell your subject, make it come alive, and pleasantly instructs through the eyes of the beholders as soon as they enter your little corner of the world. If you are not creative, go to the classroom of the veteran teacher and steal every idea you can. This benign thievery will flatter the teacher, and you will be on your way to immediately engaging the little darlings. Eventually you will get the hang of this and find your own ways to use your walls (sometimes ceilings) for teaching. There are some wonderful places to go and ways of doing things in an inexpensive manner.

Considering a teacher's salary, finding such sources is invaluable. Try visiting the neighborhood garage sales or local flea market, the dollar store, or fabric store (head for the $1 a yard table). You'll find items for the bulletin board or wall or window treatments and other accessories to distinguish your room. Students really love pretty things. Human beings gravitate toward the aesthetically pleasing, but it does not have to be expensive.

YOUR IDEAS:

The Instructional Board

The instructional board is usually a whiteboard, or "smartboard" these days, though the old-fashioned chalkboard may still be around in some schools. Make good use of whatever kind is in your room. The afternoon before your first day, and before class starts every Monday, have the entire week's assignments on the board (see Figure 1.1). The top left-hand corner is a functional place. It is visible and out of the way of any other use that you may have for that instructional board. Make sure to date each assignment so you can refer to it at a glance. This helps you and the students to have an immediate reminder of the path forward. It eliminates excuses (theirs) and confusion (yours and theirs).

This clear and predictable way of communicating assignments will always be a positive thing for you and your students. In addition, this assists with absent students. You will find they invariably return to the class and ask, "What did I miss yesterday? Did you do anything?" Please remember all you were taught about sarcasm and quell the impulse to reply, "No, we

MON 8/7	Read pp. 10–15. Journal your thoughts. Today's Topics: What are your thoughts on war? (Write for 10 minutes)
TUES 8/8	Be prepared for discussion of theocracy.
WED	
THURS	
FRI	
NO SCHOOL MON 8/14	

Figure 1.1 Sample assignments for the week.

were waiting for you to wander back to class so we could resume learning the theory of relativity." I would talk privately and ask them, not in a mean fashion, what was wrong that caused their absence. If they were not at a funeral or hospital, I asked them what schoolwork they had done while absent. Reminding them that the syllabus, given at the beginning of the term, was for occasions like these so they could plan ahead or catch up if absent. You can also refer to the current week's assignment on the board. If you do not have a board of any kind, invest in a very large sheet of paper and tape or tack it to whatever is holding up the ceiling (tree, column).

YOUR IDEAS:

Another way you may consider using this space is to have an assignment posted on the board every day, which the students are to begin immediately upon entering the classroom. Of course, the type of assignment depends upon age and subject matter, but even nonreaders can be given an assignment. The sample assignments can be found on page 80.

Most important to know is the value of this strategy. If you condition the students to expect daily assignments that require them to get right to work, you will find the noise level in the class is minimal, raucous behavior extinguished, and academic focus immediately puts them in a mindset from which you can springboard into the day's lesson.

I also highly recommend that tranquil background music be played during this time, such as Bach, Mozart, Gershwin, easy jazz, lilting tunes from the Irish hills, etc. Studies regarding the positive impact of music in a learning environment are very interesting. You may want to investigate. I found it to always be beneficial. However, it may take students a little time to embrace the concept and your music choices. Typically, at least one student will ask about the music and request "their" music be played. Though I understand the motivation for such a request, I believe during reading and writing activities all are best served with soothing and mind-freeing music. Popular music is not in any way being disrespected simply because an informed decision is being made by the professional: that's you. Do not try to get into a discussion or justification of your decision. The use of this music is based upon educational knowledge and experience. It is appropriate to make a statement that perhaps incorporating student music in an upcoming project would be feasible.

Side Note

Setting up plastic milk crates designated for each class, or perhaps by subject, is one of the most efficient ways to provide access to handouts (syllabus, rules, calendar, etc.). When a student or parent needs replacement information, it is right at your fingertips. I saw one teacher do this, but this person also had a file folder for each student's graded tests. Instead of sending the graded tests home, he sent a form:

Subject: _____	Teacher: _____	Date: _____
Student: _____	Material covered: _____	
Grade: _____	Parent signature: _____	

This form was returned to the teacher who stapled it to the test and put in student file folder.

At the end of the semester or year, the teacher had a documented way to justify the student's progress. It is sad but true that you must devise methodology to assure you can substantiate the grade the student earns. This also provides you with information about what needs to be reviewed post testing.

One last word about instructional boards. Any daily information you need on the board, get it up there before they come in or have a student write the information or assignment. Do not turn your back to the class. Just do not. Even as a mother of three with a good set of eyes in the back of my head, I had some trouble a few times. In the best of classes there is always one little "Damien." There is always the mischievous student ready to derail the day with a spit ball, ugly hand gesture, etc. That takes time and attention from your daily goal. This is just a word to the wise; some things never change!

Room Arrangement

The arrangement of the furniture has always been something that amazes me. I am amazed because I have been in rooms where all furniture has been in the same place for years. I do realize not everyone is comfortable out of the box, but this is one area where I implore you to get out of the box. Create a learning environment where learning can occur and consider something other than rows. Think about what your goals are. You want to disseminate information, but more, you want them to take it in, gobble it up, ingest it, and not just regurgitate it. Even college level classrooms would benefit from the creative arrangement of furniture. Do you want discussion in the class? They need to see and hear each other, possibly a circle or a square. Do you want collaboration occurring, possible pods of three or four desks. Desks are useful at times, mandatory even, but consider all the possibilities when you look at your space.

While teaching a variety of language arts and theater classes, my classrooms ranged from the dreaded trailer, to the lunchroom, the home economics room—all kinds of spaces, big, small, hot, cold, and one with a persistent leak. Some days I would even put desks in the hall for the period if I did not need them, and then drag them back inside the room afterwards. Do not hesitate to involve the students in helping you with the "classroom shuffle." Most of them are very willing. Administrators are not always on board with the innovative teacher, but they should be.

Examples of survival are endless. The bottom line is this: Make your room yours and make it work for the students. The best administrator I ever had said, "If it is good for the student, that is what we are going to do" (Brenda Colby, South Forsyth High School, Cumming, GA).

The last consideration regarding the physical space you have is be safe. Tell your kids where safety information is posted. Make sure it is large enough for someone to actually read it a few feet away. You need exit and other procedural information about fire, tornado, hurricane, bomb threat, and anything else relative to your geographic area and today's troubled times. I believe it would be good to demonstrate the Heimlich maneuver for people choking.

It would be very worthwhile to have a little discussion the first week of school about the gravity of emergencies and the need for everyone to exhibit a particular type of behavior. List them on the board and talk about it. You will not know initially where your children are coming from in terms of their own frightening experiences or total lack of, and it is essential that you establish a climate of safety and trust. This is another opportunity for you to really get to know your students better, and perhaps for them to recognize the similar experiences or feelings of their fellow students. Such moments will always serve to enhance the general climate of trust. Students must believe you take their safety seriously, and that you are strong and definitely in control during those times.

Stay creative and remember your goal to give them the message: I am here to teach, I expect you to learn. P.S. I care about you.

HOW WOULD YOU LIKE YOUR ROOM TO LOOK?

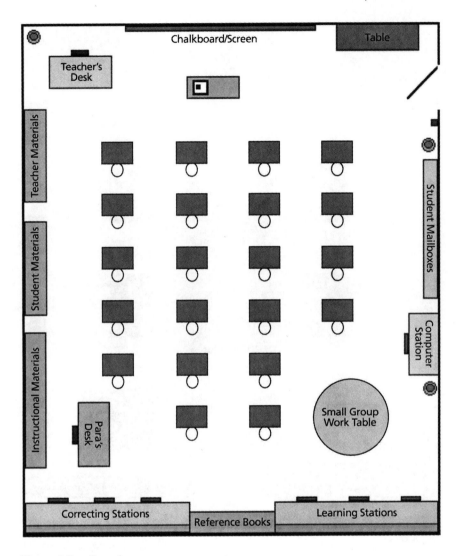

Figure 1.2a Sample room arrangement.

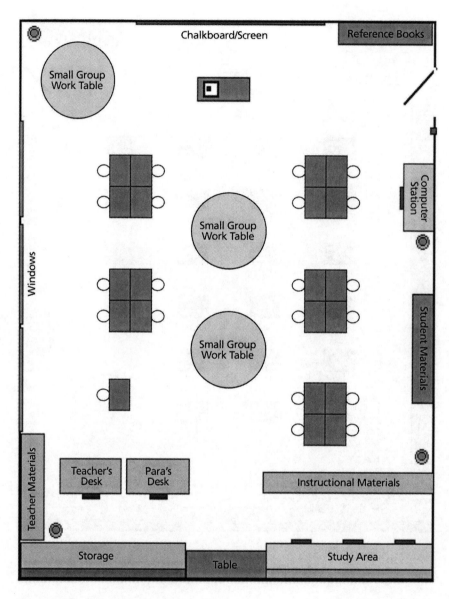

Figure 1.2b Sample room arrangement.

DRAW A SECOND POSSIBLE CLASSROOM IN WHICH YOU CAN SEE YOURSELF TEACHING EFFECTIVELY

The Seating Chart

A little aside about the seating chart: Some people do it alphabetically. That takes away any sense of bias and challenges such as, "Why did you put me here?" You may also consider setting it up alternating gender. For the younger children this may be very effective. Do give consideration to height and size, especially in middle school where growth hormones go awry. Of course, this means setting up a temporary chart. If you are going to make changes, try to make them before the second or third day and implement as they enter the following day. You will find whenever you make changes, especially among the students 12 and up, that they may try to make a scene to protest and challenge your position as the teacher. Be prepared with your confident smile and no-negotiating-but-kind voice.

I believe strongly in the seating chart because it sends a clear message that you are in control, and that you are fair but clear about why people sit where. It says that you took the time to organize and prepare for them. This is a strong message to human beings, and even very young students perceive this on some level. (If you have never read *The Children's Story* by James Clavell, take an hour and do so. You will never forget it.) Can you recall going somewhere, invited or expected, and they were not prepared for you?

Do tell students that you may decide to adjust the seat assignments as becomes necessary. Therefore, this little piece of paper that appears so small in your hand turns out to be very important. If you are reading this and are clueless about a seating arrangement for your class, run, do not walk, to the most experienced teacher you can find and ask them about how you do one. Make copies of your seating chart and update as necessary. You should have one taped to your desk and taped to the podium, as well as one in your "current" substitute folder, one in your grade book, and a couple of loose ones you can grab. Why the hysteria about "the chart?" It is because it has their names on it. Until you know their names, you will not be in control of that class and they know it. You may be looking at trying to remember 110–130 names at the beginning of every semester if you are in high school, fewer if you are teaching college, fewer if you are in the middle school arena, and even fewer if you are in elementary. If you don't understand the passion a person has about his or her name, read John Proctor's monologue in act 5 of Arthur Miller's *The Crucible*.

Sample Seating Chart

Remember it will be a work in progress until you find what works best for each student. He or she may have specific needs that require a seat to accommodate those needs.

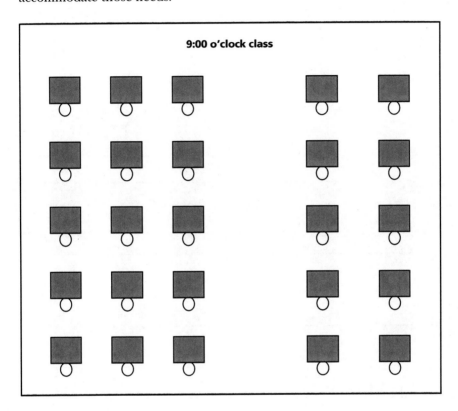

9:00 o'clock class

YOUR IDEAS?

It is the supreme
art of the teacher
to awaken joy in
creative expression.

—Albert Einstein

The Substitute

This is really, really important: the substitute situation.

When you first begin, you cannot imagine ever being absent and turning your little students over to a substitute. Time will pass and you may daydream about giving your charges over to Broomhilda the Hun who would make the students appreciate you. Somewhere between the two mindsets is reality. So here are some brief and very wise points.

Immediately find out how the sub system works in your town/county/township. Do you call a sub and beg? Does central office do this? Can you request a particular one? Find this out the first week (from the best veteran teacher). It is almost unheard of for you to get to plan to be out. It happens when your youngest child breaks a nose catching a softball (with her nose) thrown by another 5th-grade girl waiting to be recruited by the Yankees. It happens when your elder daughter calls crying with mastitis as she holds her squalling 3-week-old baby girl saying, "Momma, can you come?" It is the unexpected.

So, here is what you do. Have a notebook that says The Substitute. Inside you have:

- Page 1: Administrators names and phone extensions
- Page 2: General rules of the particular school
- Page 3: Class rules and discipline for infractions
- Page 4: Current seating chart. If you have been innovative and the kids say, "That isn't the way we have been doing it." The response is: "This is the way we are doing it until Mrs./Ms./Mr. _____ returns. Get into the appropriate seat. Now."
- Page 5: List a page number and sentence or two from the last quarter of your text (unless it is math or science, in which case you need to get creative and come up with something that is definitely challenging). Assure students this will be collected within a specific period, will be graded, and will probably have a weighty effect on their GPRs.

Intimidation? You bet. You just hope the best sub has been called in (chances of this are slim to none). Sorry, nothing easy or pretty about being absent. Try to find out from the veteran teachers who the best subs are and try to get them called for you.

In the end, unlike many other careers in the world, being absent is not only a pain to prepare for, but can be an absolute catastrophe. From day one, if your students believe you are a person of your word and that your word is law, the outcome will be manageable. They will all try you, but once you are out and then return and hold them to account, things will be a little smoother.

One more thing: If they act out outrageously, you must bring the hammer down. Then revaluate what you left for the sub and amend to improve for a better outcome. Speaking directly with the sub is advised.

Yet another thing: Do include in your initial parent communication a statement relating to the required behavior of a student when the teacher is not in attendance, and the subsequent response. It may or may not cover some parental whining if their child is reprimanded for misbehavior in the absence of the teacher. Sad you have to cover all potential situations, but you do.

PART **2**

The Importance of Others

The mediocre teacher tells. The good teacher explains. The superior teacher demonstrates. The great teacher inspires.

—William A. Ward

2

The Importance of Others

Kindness is never wasted. If you want some,
you had better give some.

—SCB

Support Staff

One of the first alliances you need to make is with the janitorial staff. Recognize from the get-go that these people can make or break your teaching success. Preposterous you say? Think again. Who is going to empty your trash, sweep and mop the room, or clean up after a sick child leaves breakfast on the floor? Who is going to let you in when you leave your keys in your class and everyone else is gone and you have to get some material prepared before class tomorrow? If you feel you are above these staff members, you are wrong. They are part and parcel of the school family. They usually are from the community and know it much better than you know. They know many of the kids and might even give you some insight about a few. They usually see things you and others overlook. I have had some of the most interesting and even encouraging discussions with these men and women

Control Is NOT a Four Letter Word, pages 31–34
Copyright © 2017 by Information Age Publishing
All rights of reproduction in any form reserved.

before and after school. Take the time to find out their names and who they are. You won't be sorry. While you are at it, make sure students always treat these auxiliary personnel with respect and consideration.

The other people you need to get to know are the counselors and the front office staff. Get to really know them and let them know you. (Un-expected doughnuts or bagels are a good way to make sure they remem-ber you.) Always say good morning and always ask them how they are. Be prepared to stop and listen to their responses. You will be amazed at the in-school professional network that emerges just that simply. Though I be-lieve that one should greet all people in that manner, sometimes as you are rushing through the counseling department or front office, the social ame-nities are lost.The last but not least important support person you need to ingratiate yourself with is the technology department the on or off campus people. Do what it takes: doughnuts, coffee, gift certificates, whatever.

The purpose for all of this is for your students. Unfortunately, it seems that everybody is busy in the educational system, and if you think your pay-check is low, you need to know the counselors are the same and the office staff is less. There will be times when you need these people to really hear you, not for yourself, but your students. If the people outside of your class-room know you to be kind and caring and "all about your kids," you will be treated in a kind and caring fashion. If you begin by being demanding and impatient about things that you cannot even imagine now and that they control, your students will not be as well served.

Peers

Obviously, it is important that the relationship with your peers is good. Ap-plauding your peers' successes, picking their brains for solutions, and main-taining a sense of humor will go a long way toward helping you stay strong and focused on your job of controlling your class and successfully imparting information. Get out of your own department every now and then and see what is happening with them. This kind of friendliness is often contagious, and it cannot help but have a positive impact within the school community.

You cannot be as effective in your role as teacher if you are unprofes-sional when interacting with your peers. Do not ever talk about another person—administrator, teacher, janitor, or student—in a disparaging way. Ever. Your peers, students, and support personnel will lose respect for you and they most assuredly will not trust you. That will ultimately manifest itself in classroom behavior.

My grandfather, a stately southern gentleman of few words, left me with sage advice when he said, "A person who talks to you about someone else, will be talking about you when you walk out of the room."

Administrators

The last group, but certainly the most powerful to consider when thinking about how you are going to control your class, are the administrators. They control your fate: what classes you are going to teach, how many students you will have, where your classroom is located, when your planning period will be. Generally, their decisions are not personal.

I worked under seven or eight principals, and for a while I lost count and heart. I have to tell you I have seen the good, the bad, the ugly, the mean, the sweet, the best dressed, the most fun, the slow, the quick, and everything in-between from the ultraprofessional to tobacco chewing ex-coaches. (Hmmmm. Is ex-coach an oxymoron?)

Principals can make your life miserable or they can make you whistle all the way to work.

(It may be obvious that I could write at least a short book on principals, but that might end in a lawsuit.)

The bottom line about administrators is:

- Find out what they are about
- Use that information for the betterment of your kids
- Give whatever time and attention to the powers that be so you can get the best and most for your students. Note: Keep your relationship with them strictly professional. Do not chat with them casually about concerns in or out of the classroom, except in a professional venue. Yes, there is a story behind this advice.

To be real good at this, you need to watch your veteran teachers: what works and does not, and how it changes with each principal. It is hard every time you have a new one come in, but take the time to get to know what you can expect of them and what they will expect of you.

Believe me, the size of your class does affect control. The location of your class (trailers are my biggest peeve) can set the tone for behavior that you have to fight to change. Being given a subject to teach two days before school opens does happen, and you just have to suck it up and know you are going to be running a chapter ahead of the students all year.

All these decisions will be made or approved by the primary administrator, so your relationship with them is very important.

Actually, you can have a wonderful professional relationship with all staff members. However, remember you are not more or less important because of your duties and responsibilities, and neither is anyone else.

Appropriate socializing can even be a part of your job and enhance communication, but ultimately everyone still needs to be clear about his or her job description and understand that decisions should always be made for the good of the students.

YOUR THOUGHTS:

PART **3**

Getting Ahead of the Game

I am not a teacher—but an awakener.

—Robert Frost

3

Getting Ahead of the Game

Organizing and Utilizing the Written Word

This is going to be more interesting
than it sounds.

Textbooks

Day One

I can hear the groans as you read this heading. We are going to deal with practical things no one told you about as you skipped blithely through the graduation line and on to human resources in some educational building. Filling out forms, you will find, was the least of beginning your new job. So what can I say about textbooks, at least that anyone cares to hear? Though I was never a very good teacher from textbooks, they do have their place and some subjects simply have to use it as a guide. After the first few years, even I learned to recognize the positive side of having a textbook. Though I am going to use the term textbooks, let us understand that we are referring to any type of learning material that is loaned or given to students

Control Is NOT a Four Letter Word, pages 39–48
Copyright © 2017 by Information Age Publishing

and that you will be dispensing. With so much change annually within the school systems, it is difficult to identify specifically what you will be required to handle. All the more reason to identify this as early as possible.

Taking First Things First

You have to get them from the storage room to your classroom. That storage room might be next door to your classroom or across campus in the bowels of another building altogether. Typically, materials I needed always seemed to be far away when I was teaching. If you do not have a dolly at your disposal that you can bring from home, look throughout the school for some way to roll your textbooks and other materials to your room.

Interestingly enough, a rather ugly phenomenon can occur the day everyone is trying to get materials. I have seen fairly literate, genteel women, and otherwise polite men elbow each other out of their way to get first possession of something with wheels. It might actually be a dolly or even your teacher desk chair, but more than likely a cart from the media center. (The media specialist: Did you remember to make friends with this person? Make a note, they are very important people and unfortunately might be a bit puffed up with power on opening day when everyone wants one of their carts.) If you can get in the school's storage closets the day before everyone else shows up, everything will be much easier.

Here's the picture you strive for:

- All texts (workbooks, etc.) stacked up at the front of your classroom.
- You have your class rolls.
- You have computer-generated or hand-constructed charts for each class or group of children you expect with each student's name (alphabetized). The seating chart.
- The following goes hand in hand with the seating chart I recommended. Write the student's name who will sit in that desk on an index card taped to the top of the desk. If you have more than one class period, list the period number on the index card and the student's name for each period.
- Color code the index cards for each class: e.g., Row 1, Seat 1— First class, pink card, John Brown; Second class, blue card, Alice Ames; Third class, yellow card, George Akers.
- Put one text on each desk. You will make a written note of the identifying text number beside the name of the student, but in pencil. It needs to be erasable.

Handouts

Next, you need to have all handouts printed, counted, and stacked. I recommend color coding by period or by subject matter, and placed in ascending or descending order for the day or time that you will be dispersing them. Place them on your desk, which should be free of everything except materials for that first day. Or if you are lucky, you may have a good-sized table upon which you can place these items. A word about handouts: You'll have to buy your own colored paper and probably many other things. Keep a file for your receipts of job-related expenditures. You may be able to write them off on your taxes. Keep mileage and gas expenses also.

Do not wait until the week before to generate the masters for your handouts. Murphy's Law swings into full force when you are coming up to the deadline of first day, and I have seen some very brave souls buckle when their computer crashes the day before school opens, and the line is so long at the school copier that joining the homeless and unemployed looks inviting.

Therefore, this is what I recommend: Make sure that you have the four most important handouts done at least two weeks before school (the masters) and have them copied a week before. Some beginning teachers or slow-learning teachers may decide they deserve to have a last summer vacation fling of 3 to 10 days (whatever) before preparing for the opening week of school. There are even some veteran teachers who may decide not to "sweat the small stuff" and mosey on in the first "required" day. Anyway, a word to the wise should be sufficient. The office personnel will be at work at least a couple of weeks before the beginning of school, although they may be working half days, but they can show you all about copying. I stress again, color code according to subject matter or class periods, if possible.

The four most important handouts:

- Attendance policy
- Behavior policy
- Grading policy
- Educational objectives (syllabus), and for the semester, the first 6 to 8 week syllabus (include major assignments)

If you are a procrastinator, you are now muffling your disdainful laughter at the need to get so organized. How hard can it be? The answer is, as hard as you make it by not getting all your materials together, and as hard as the students can make it, related to the developmental learning slot they are in and the myriad of quirks and idiosyncrasies they bring to your classroom.

The First Day

Preparation is going to pay off.

- Very soft calm music should be playing.
- Instructional board has Week at a Glance. Write the educational focus for each day and the homework for each day on the instructional board. Place it on the left hand side from top to bottom, not taking up too much space. Make it legible.
- Day's assignments are in the top center of the instructional board. Indicate how work will be evaluated and length of time for assignment.
- Note any other information they may want to know.
- Consider having a trivia question of the day for the "fast" students who finish early.

Instructional Board
(Whiteboard, Chalk, Smartboard, Paper)

Week at a Glance	TODAY'S ASSIGNMENT
Monday	WRITE A ONE-PAGE BIOGRAPHY 15 min. Graded on effort
Tuesday	
TRIVIA: What is the origin of English?	

Figure 3.1 Sample of an instructional board.

What this does for you: When you greet each student (with that sincere smiling face), you indicate where his or her desk is and point to the board (see Figure 3.1). Say something encouraging like, "I am anxious to read about you." The students immediately become engaged in productive work and you are establishing your expectations for engaged and obedient students. You have also sent a message, a powerful one: "I want to know about you. I cared enough about you to prepare for your arrival. I have high expectations of you."

This is a very powerful communication tool.

While everyone is writing, you will be able to:

- Take roll
- Clarify the assignment for some

- Make a mental note of those having trouble getting or keeping on task, maybe put a little dot beside their name so when you read their paper you have a heads-up about them as a learner
- Make written notes about what you need to do for this class before tomorrow
- Catch your breath, and when the time limit is up, collect the papers.

Establish a predictable manner for this to occur. Repetition is your friend. Contrary to some beliefs, predictability is actually a very reassuring thing, especially to young learners, but also to certain types of learners. Have them pass their paper to the front of each aisle and then the front desk students will pass to the right (or left). This is an efficient and time saving method with a modicum of noise or distraction. The last student to receive the stack of papers will then go to a designated area, place a paper clip on the stack, and place in a basket designated for that period. This will help you immensely once the day starts piling on.

Cell Phones

A little interjection here: Cell phones are from the devil. I know this because I have 10 grandchildren and 8 of them have cell phones. I have heard and I understand their absolute necessity for these young people to "function," "be safe," "stay informed," and "feel secure." Frankly, I do not buy it for one moment. If you believe any of that, you are in for a very long year. Students use cell phones in the classroom unless they think they will actually have them taken from them. It does not matter whether they are the failing student or the best student. Have a basket on your desk. Lift it up the first day and say, "If you have your phone out of your bookbag, I will put it into this basket until the end of class. If I collect it from you twice, I will keep it until your parent comes and picks it up. There will be absolutely no discussion about this issue."

Obviously, you have to know and abide by school policy. However, remember there is more than one way to skin a rabbit. Be creative and find a way to win.

TAKE 20 MINUTES AND WRITE YOUR AUTOBIOGRAPHY OR LIST THE FIVE MOST IMPORTANT DECISIONS YOU EVER MADE.

Transitioning

While you are collecting work, tell them to write tomorrow's homework assignment down. Look around. Try to make sure everyone is doing that. Also, ask how they "felt" about writing about their life? Ask why they think you asked them to write about themselves. You may get a quick response of, "Cause you want to know about us." Your response might be, "Yes, I am interested in getting to know you because we are going to be spending a lot of time together, and I want to know the best way to teach you. Knowing you will help me. Also, maybe we will have a chance to all know one another better. Learning is easier when we know and respect each other."

This is a great time to say you have a challenge. "Can anyone name every person in the class?" Have on hand a small reward appropriate for the age and class. I generally avoid sweets, but something like a cool pencil or eraser can suffice. Have limited attempts and then say, "We'll try that again tomorrow."

Moving on, this is a good time to reintroduce yourself and welcome them. Try to make direct eye contact with each as you speak. Size them up because they are definitely sizing you up. It is an important time.

Open the conversation about what is going to be taught. What is biology or what do you think you will learn in fifth grade? Try to engender comments and questions. Insert into this the method one employs to speak: The raising of the hand is generally the accepted one. Commenting on respect for the individual speaking is appropriate here. Next, tackle the rules. This should be a good time to establish the rules for the year. Specific strategies for creating the rules are in Part 5 of this book.

RECALL A CLASSROOM MOMENT WHEN YOU HAD A STRONG REACTION TO A TEACHER, POSITIVE OR NEGATIVE. DESCRIBE YOUR MEMORY.

Now back to the textbooks (this is assuming you have textbooks.)

Pass around a sheet which has each student's name listed and with a line next to it for them to record the ID number of their textbook. This is essential when you collect them in at the end of the year. Invariably books are lost. *You* are responsible for accounting for them and if you do not know who had what book, you will be explaining to your department chair or administrator why you are not returning the correct number of textbooks. This is the way to avoid that dilemma. Follow this with a general initiation to the text. This activity needs to be tailored to the age and subject matter. It is a good idea, at the very least, to have them look at the title and the author(s) and then open to the table of contents. I cannot begin to tell you how frequently I have had high school students who could not readily find that area of the text. Then have them look at the index and talk about how it could be used. You might even want to have an assignment related to the text for the first night, if time runs out before you are finished talking. Their assignment: Choose a specific term related to your subject and the first chapter topic, e.g., gravity. Tell them to look up in the index and list the pages where the term can be found.

Routine

The following days you will spend a certain period of time discussing the handouts. Make sure and establish a routine for the beginning of class. Whatever your students' ages and subject matter dictate getting a routine. You will never regret it.

WHAT ARE SOME ROUTINES YOU HAVE IN YOUR LIFE? POSITIVE? NEGATIVE?

Other Materials

Each class has a variety of needs. Each school district has a variety of needs and economic support systems. If you are at a wealthy, well-endowed school system, private or otherwise, you just figure out what you need and let your department head know. This type of school is rare. Therefore, the real inside skinny is this: I have noticed that different administrators and department heads may have different agendas than yours. Although I was always positive what I wanted for my students should be considered most important, in the cold light of retirement, I might on occasion have been wrong. (Sigh.) All that said, passion and conviction will help you in the long run, and so figure out what you:

- Must have
- Need to have
- Want to have

Go to your department head (who, by the way, may be a saint of all teachers or spawned from Satan), and try to enlist him or her in getting what you feel you must have and work down from there. Check out the media center, but you must be prepared for not having all that you want. Your options then are to:

- Enlist parents
- Beg from local stores. They are usually quite nice even if they have to say no.
- Get creative and start viewing trash (not to be confused with garbage) in a new way.
- Reach into your shallow pockets, as every teacher I have ever known has, and go shopping at the cheapest place you can find. Most stores (Staples, Office Depot, Barnes & Noble, Books a Million, etc.) give a 10% educators' break. If you beg they may give you more. If you can get in with someone and "chat them up" about the type of things you need and why, they may have some ideas to augment your own.
- Think outside the box

The following is a list of items I always tried to have in my room. Some items can be employed in a class project or on individual projects, if the student cannot afford the material. You will also find having enrichment types of materials will be very good for students who learn in different ways. Students come not only in different colors, shapes, and genders, but their brains come from lots of different paths and experiences. Some of these items might help.

- Pencils and erasers
- Ink pens
- Highlighters (different colors)
- Notebook paper
- Unlined paper
- Books pertaining to subject matter
- Magazines (to read)
- Magazines to cut
- Glue
- Poster board
- Scraps of fabric
- DVDs directly related to subject matter and preapproved by the department head or administrator
- CDs and CD player
- Butcher block paper
- Used candle, extraneous bits of wood
- Copies of master art works
- Clay
- Assortment of photographs, black and white, if possible

I liked to always have some corner where students might retreat for inspiration or sometimes just a break. So an old rocker or piece of carpet might be useful. Once I tried a couple of beanbags. There is a reason you do not see them much. An inventive and determined child can find a way to puncture the vinyl. I leave you with your imagination.

The best teachers
are those who show
you where to look,
but don't tell you
what to see.

—Alexandra Trenfor

PART **4**

Time Is Not Your Friend

What you leave behind is not what is engraved in stone monuments, but what is woven into the lives of others.

—Pericles

4

Time Is Not Your Friend

Overview

Now you are in the classroom and you have just about everything you need—except time. I used to have different sayings all over my walls, and sometimes if we needed to have a 5 or 10 minute "sponge activity," we would write or discuss one of the quotes posted on the walls.

My favorite was, "Time is not my friend." You would be surprised how many students jumped right in on this one. I had not really considered it from their point of view. A lesson for the teacher that day.

Anyway, there are many strategies for time conservation. If you remain committed to being prepared every day for school, your life will be much better. Additionally, though you need to discover techniques for evaluating student work in a timely fashion, the question here is how does grading or evaluation affect behavior? It impacts it tremendously. The student's attitude about himself or herself and you is directly related to how he or she perceives they are doing in class. This is true for all ages and subject matters.

That perception colors their behavior. One student's behavior impacts the group and here comes the old domino effect again.

A few ideas, but your peers will have many also. Ask them.

Establish Evaluation Methods

■ Establish your evaluation methods and interpretation at the very beginning.
■ Clarify the grading scale. Identify how letter grades are related to numerical grades.
  – Give examples on the board and encourage questions. All of this should be in an initial handout that both parents and students read and sign, and you file and keep 4 years.
■ Explain that behavior is a component of their grades.
  – Behavior *can* and *should* (In my opinion) be a component of the students' grade. However, you need to clearly consider *your* realistic expectations related to age and subject matter. Then you must assign a *realistic* amount (1%–5%) that will be added to the final grade. Very importantly, you must identify *how* you will evaluate each student. Keep it simple. Establish perhaps three areas that you will be observing students, for example:
    • attention in class
    • adherance to class rules
    • attitude toward others
  Tell them they each start out with 100 points (weighted perhaps as a quiz grade) and with each observed infraction they lose a point.

  (I must add a little secret that I found worked for almost all aged students. Establish the fact that you have an *actual* grade book. If someone is acting out, you very pointedly walk to your desk—don't say a word. Pick up *the grade book*, turn dramatically to the class, look at the offending student(s) and record something in *the* book. Do not smile. No comment. Continue the class.)

  Eventually you will work out the best system for you and your class, but if you are just beginning the journey of teaching, be kind to yourself and recognize it takes time. It might take a coupe of years to perfect "your best" approach, but you *will* get there.

Discuss Timeframes

- Be consistent about the length of time you allow yourself, and do not whine about how much you have to do. When something serious and unpredictable comes up, simply tell the class and give another time to expect their work returned. You will always have more to do than time permits, but you will learn some ways to use your time wisely. (FYI: I found students grading each others' papers has more problems than not.)
- Be reasonable about the amount of time the students have to prepare for an evaluation.

Identify and Explain Categories of Assessment

- Identify categories of evaluations and their weight. Most school systems have the weights in place and you will need to know and apply to exams, tests, quizzes, and daily work.
- Clarify how each assignment will be identified as having the weight of one of those previously mentioned. For example, a homework assignment might only have the weight of a daily grade, but another homework project might have the weight of a test.

The Evaluation

It took me years to feel competent in this area. Though there were classes that introduced me to testing (essay, completion, matching, etc.), I was slow to figure out that a test is an evaluation not just of the student, but also the class as a whole and the teacher. Yep, that would be you. Again I suggest you talk with the experienced teachers in your subject area or grade level. Of course your school system should provide you with the educational objectives for your subject/grade level. Department chairs are also supposed to assist you, but sometimes they are inundated with their own class responsibilities as well as the ones as chair.

Today in the current technology-dominated classrooms, there is a serious challenge of the how to evaluate. Quite candidly, I do not have the experience or technological expertise to address this important and challenging situation. I am sure between the professional classroom teacher and the dedicated technological experts, answers will be found. I hope they hurry. The classroom teacher does not need one more job on his or her instructional plate.

Embrace Benevolent Dictatorship

Generally I believe encouraging students to understand that the class will be run on democratic principles is just asking for trouble. Of course I am sure that many will not agree. Certainly that is the right of the individual. However I must tell you, after a lifetime of living and working with children birth to 21, I simply think it is a mistake. Students come to you from many environments, with a myriad of experiences (good and bad), a variety of mental and physical characteristics, and a plethora of expectations of you and the classroom. But I believe what they need is to be validated. That can be simple or not, but I think the first introduction to the class should be positive. The student should be welcomed into a clean, orderly class by a friendly person who looks happy to meet them. It is comforting, in my opinion and experience, that one person needs to be in charge. I believe that is the teacher, but I do believe in a benevolent dictator.

Teaching is an intense, challenging endeavor and yet one of the most rewarding things I have experienced.

—Teaching Fellow

PART **5**

Behavior

Believe while others doubt
Plan while others are playing
Study while others are sleeping
Decide while others are delaying
Prepare while others are dreaming
Begin while others procrastinate

—William Ward

5

Behavior

It Will Make You or Break You

Behavior is, according to Webster, the way one acts or conducts oneself. So as we approach this topic, the point must be made that we are not talking just about the behavior of the student, but also the behavior of the teacher. We generally assume we are talking about bad behavior. We are also talking about good behavior. It will be time well spent if you chat with people who really know you about your behavior: positive and negative. Lao-Tzu says, "It is wisdom to know others; it is enlightenment to know one's self." Such introspection will make you much more effective if maintaining discipline in your class.

Control Is NOT a Four Letter Word, pages 65–73
Copyright © 2017 by Information Age Publishing

JOT DOWN A FEW POSITIVE THINGS ABOUT YOUR BEHAVIOR.
CONSIDER THE DIFFERENCE BETWEEN IN AND OUT OF CLASS BEHAVIOR

Out of class

In class

Your behavior in class will directly impact the behavior of your students. Think hard about this and be aware of your strengths and your shortcomings.

Getting back to the students. What you must know from the very beginning is what realistic expectations are according to a variety of factors. What are your thoughts/beliefs of the factors listed (Figure 5.1)?

Gender

Age

Mental age

Emotional age

Social age

Social dynamics in play

Classroom experience

Figure 5.1 List your beliefs about these factors.

Hmm. Tall order? Yep. However here is the thing: It is part of your job. You cannot begin to be successful as a teacher until you understand all aspects of your student population. Teaching math, language arts, music, or science? Great, but you are not teaching anything until you have the areas listed in Figure 5.1 covered. You should have had at least one class in developmental psychology. Unfortunately, as I recall, that class was early on in my educational process, and I do not remember a lot of emphasis on its relevance. Maybe there was. You may have had some very good classes in cognition, and maybe even social considerations of the learner. Whatever your educational experience beforehand, here are a few suggestions:

- Once you know the grade level, research information on charac-teristics of your future learners.
- You must know and come to understand the demographics of your students.
- Ask a veteran teacher of the same age group (and hopefully subject area) if you can observe his or her classroom, and not just one time. Every day is different.
- See if there are any DVDs recorded of classes that emphasize the study of behavior.
- Go to the counselor and show her your class rolls. Are there any students that he or she can identify who you should be looking out for, to assist in any special way? Clarification: You are not ask-ing for privileged information, you are simply trying to get info that you will know by the end of the year anyway, but by then the students will be on their way out of the class and you may never have them as students again.

Warning: In the faculty lounge, lunchroom, halls, or bleachers you will encounter jaded teachers who should never have come to the classroom or should have quit once they started disliking students. These groups will bad-mouth the kids, the administration, their peers, and you when you walk away. It is so sad when you see that there are more than a few, and they have such a negative impact on individuals who look to them for an education. If a student was pointed out as a bad kid, I immediately started investigating the kid's real story. Usually the results were that there was a real need in the student's life. Typically, this was the student who I could trust most, once he learned he could trust an adult.

- Go to the department of special education. You need to identify students who need special services. There may be one made available to you. There may not. So you go to the special education department. If there isn't one, go to the primary administrator and ask what's up. Every school is different, but you must be assertive and find out how things are done and how you can serve your student appropriately. There is a plethora of rules and guidelines related to these students. They may have cognitive learning issues from low IQ to genius, ADD, ADHD, dyslexic, dysgraphic, (the list is endless) mobility difficulties, coordination problems, and emotional dysfunction. Before the first day you must have this information. Consult with the individual teachers who handle each file and try to get a plan in place ASAP.

■ One more really important thing. Know what the county and school rules are about the major areas:
  − Attendance
  − Tardiness
  − Makeup work. It's really important that you are totally in line with the department, school, and county. Kids and parents are masters at manipulating the system if everyone is not on the same page, frequently wearing you down.
  − Cheating, including *plagiarism* (lots of that going on these days)
  − Exceptions that override teacher mandated rules. You may be surprised at this, but it happens. You need to know ahead of time in order to head off any unnecessary, going-to-lose-anyway battles and find a way around it. This kind of information will probably be learned in the faculty lounge. Do not take it as the total truth until you have checked it out with the most respected teacher in the school.
  − Violence
  − Bullying
  − Disrespect to faculty and staff
  − Disrespect to fellow students
  − Disrespect of school property
  − Absence at school functions related to a grade (band, theater, etc.)
  − Fill in if you think I missed something

TABLE 5.1 What Do You Think Are Appropriate Policies for Each of These Infractions?

Attendance
Tardiness
Makeup work
Cheating
Bullying
Violence
Disrespect to school property
Disrespect to faculty / staff
Disrespect to fellow students
Absence at school function related to a class grade
Exceptions by administration overriding teacher

Your Class Rules

There seems to be a few basic mindsets regarding the class rules. Each has its own particular chance of success, and unfortunately failure.

The Democratic Approach

Give the darlings "ownership." They may respond to this high-minded idea. If there is a student able to write suggestions on the board, appoint one. If you need to do the recording, make sure and do not turn your back completely to the class. There will be a tendency, once they all get their creative juices flowing, to come up with a multitude of rules (I am talking 20 to 30), which range from do not ask to go to the restroom more than once an hour, or to the obvious, such as do not talk in class. The younger the student, the more the rules. They still think school is pretty cool, and to be able to say something out loud and get it written on the board—wow. The older ones will be more discerning and try to make the rules work for them. In other words, manipulation of the teacher to sabotage the day's lessons. In my opinion, the democratic concept in a school setting is fraught with pitfalls, but if you "believe" in this, give it a try.

Here are some guidelines:

- Announce you will be writing everybody's ideas down and then a few will be chosen.
- Agree on a specified number and stick to it. Establish accepted discipline measures for transgressors.
- Write them down also and stick to them.

The Dictatorship Approach

The no choice, like-it-or-lump-it approach. Frequently this approach is tolerated relatively well, which is not always good because it means, if they are young, they think they have no choice so they do not make any noise about it one way or another. Not really the message you want to give. The older ones may be hardened and do not plan to pay much attention to them one way or another. Such indifference and negative approach to class order needs to be addressed immediately. Here is where your time and attention before the first day of school in identifying a variety of aspects about your students is so vital.

The Benevolent Dictatorship

This is my preferred approach. Bring a little humor, steeled with sincere commitment. I think you should tell the class up front exactly what you expect and why it is imperative. Respect needs to be mentioned early. Maybe having someone define the word will help.

I believe in treating them as intelligent human beings who have a very real stake in the way the class is run. This is the time (first day) where you have "the talk." Establish first how group discussions must go (raise hand, only one speaking at a time, etc.). We know Robert's Rules of Order will not emerge from this discussion, but tailor it to the situation. In other words, use common sense and guide them toward that goal. Tell them frankly (and you need to already know what the rules need to be) that the most important thing you care about is that they are safe in the room, and that you want each student individually to learn important things during his or her time with you. The question needs to be prompted by, "What is important to each of you?" Truly, this can be very revealing to you and them, and maybe even have a few surprises in store for everyone. Initiate your scribe function at this point with something like, "In this class, I will ask students to write on the board when we are talking and need to remember what is being said. Would someone like to volunteer? Please raise your hand."

If no one volunteers, you will hopefully have identified a confident student you can expect to willingly approach the front of the class. If no one does, ask two students you think are up to the task to write them and then read them back to the class. For the nonreaders have some large visuals (stick figures even) of students showing right behavior and wrong behavior. Have the class indicate which is right/wrong, e.g., writing at the desk, throwing wadded paper, eating a candy bar, covertly sitting and listening attentively, pushing a student, or helping a student up from a fall. Tape correct behavior pictures on the board.

If this is your first class and you are prepared up to this point, relax and trust your instincts. If the student chosen has totally unintelligible writing, let them write one idea and then ask for another volunteer. Note of caution: Generally girls will always have better handwriting (it's that small motor thing). But do not have someone in front of the class who may be dressed in such a way that he or she becomes the show. Times have changed, and besides remember you are the star of the show.

Class Motto

Suggested class motto to display in a prominent area of the room.

- Respect rules of this class
- Respect your fellow students
- Respect the teacher
- Respect yourself

One year I laminated a huge banner that stretched across the instructional board:

Respect... Responsibility... Resourcefulness

The first day of class we developed our class rules based upon these words. A great activity that bore much good fruit.

Basing the rules not so much on the no talking, no bullying, no...no...no..., but instead on what positive behavior is expected and how everyone benefits from this approach, I believe is more effective. However, I have to admit you will always have a student (maybe two or three) who just will defy you. You need to make a quick study and try to get this under control right away. It will require an immediate conversation with the student, the parent, the counselor, maybe even the administrator. Most of the time there is a significant "story" that accompanies the student. You will need to make a plan right away. Wishing, hoping, or praying will not resolve this problem. Regardless of the reason the troubled and defiant student has, it is never okay for the other 99% to be deprived of a calm, orderly, and stimulating learning environment.

WHAT HAVE YOU SEEN THAT WORKS?

WHAT HAVE YOU SEEN THAT DOESN'T WORK?

good teacher can
inspire hope, ignite the
imagination, and instill
a love of learning.

—Brad Henry

PART 6

Resources

What sculpture is
to a block of marble,
education is to a
human soul.

—Joseph Addison

6

Resources

The 20-Minute Presentation

Typically, spending a maximum of 20 minutes per activity is recommended. You might consider structuring an activity like the following:

- Introduction to the topic: Ask a leading question, which hopefully causes them to remember anything they may know about the subject. Be prepared that initially they may not know or recognize that they know anything about the topic. Have them jot their thoughts or experience related to the topic on their paper.
- Definition of the topic: Have the definition on the board, but covered. Uncover definition. Have a student read it. Ask for reactions. What do they understand? How does this relate to any prior knowledge? Does it make sense?
- Relate definition to something in their world. Of course, this is related specifically to the learner's age, experience, and abilities.

- Restatement by the students: Clarification by the teacher if necessary.
- Writing: Cover your definition on the board and ask the students to write their definitions. Then uncover definition and have them write your definition. Have them compare theirs and yours.
- Application: Whatever the topic, after personal relating move on to relating it to the broader academic picture. How does this topic relate to the student's world?
- Free write: Put all notes away, or turn over and do not refer to them. Erase any relevant notes on the board. Remove definition from sight. Write for 5 minutes. Turn in to the teacher.

Developing the ability to engage in free write can empower students in the most amazing ways: Confidence in their memory, writing, thinking, and trust of their peers and teacher.

Take a break. Stand and stretch or go to the restroom. Take 5 to 10 minutes before going on to another aspect of the day's educational agenda.

Suggested Writing Assignments

Making writing a part of your everyday routine, especially the first month, will reap a multitude of positive things:

- It focuses the entire class on an individually controlled activity.
- It provides students with the opportunity to calm their inner voice and direct it toward what you believe to be a priority of the day—known by many as the educational objective.
- Consider and list a variety of topics or concepts related to your subject matter. Construct and create as many writing topics as possible. This will get easier as you have more experience.

Get to Know Your Students (By Grade Level)

General

- Tell me about yourself (a brief biography). (2–12)
- Describe your room at home. (2–12)
- Describe the most important thing, person, place, or event in your life. (2–12)
- Explain what you want to do when you grow up. (2–12)
- What is the one thing of which you are most proud? (4–12)

- What are you afraid of? (2–12)
- Describe how you feel about this room. (2–12)
- Who is the most important person to you? (2–12)

Language Arts

- Describe something in this room. (2–HS)
- Tell me about your most favorite thing to do. (2–8)
- Describe the most enjoyable thing you have ever done. (4–8)
- What is the last book you read and tell me what you did or did not enjoy? (4–9)
- Explain how to do something. (7–12)
- Discuss the most important "life choice" you have ever made. (9–12)

Science

- What is the most difficult thing to understand about water? (4–8)
- Describe air. (4–12)
- Explain gravity. (4–12)
- How do you feel about the subject of science? (4–12)

History

- Explain what history is. (4–12)
- What is the importance of studying history? (4–12)
- Describe your neighborhood, town, or city. (2–12)
- Who is the most important person in history? (4–12)
- What is the most important thing that has happened in the history of the world, America, or your town? (4–12)

Art or Music

- What is your favorite kind of art activity?
- What are the different kinds of art? (4–12)
- Who is your favorite artist and why? (7–12)
- What is your favorite kind of music? Describe it. (6–12)
- What musical instrument do you play or wish you could play and why? (4–12)
- Tell me everything you know about theater. (4–12)
- Why are the arts valuable to society? (9–12)

The first day establishes a routine of writing. Explain how much time they will have to complete the task. Tell them the only grade will be a "completion" grade, and you will read and respond to each thing they write. Do not panic. This is possible. Pace yourself and develop a grading strategy. For example, write on the board the first day that the writing grading system will be:

check + = 100 (✓+)
check = 90 (✓)
check – = 80 (✓–)
no check– = 70
and no writing = 0

Educational Objectives

- Increase fluency
- Familiarize student with the comfort of the process of writing
- Establish trust student to student and student to teacher

YOUR THOUGHTS, CONCERNS:

Trust Exercises

It is imperative that an environment of trust is established in the class-room as soon as possible. This is becoming increasingly difficult in today's schools. You can try to head off problems by immediately attending to this need. Here are a few things you can do.

Have a clock visible to the students, or hold your watch up where they can see it and say, "You are going to have 2 minutes to complete the following task. You may not speak. Separate yourselves into groups by eye color. Go."

Follow up: Congratulate them on completing the task and tell them you have another task. "Again, without talking, put yourself in groups according to hair color. Go." If you have a majority with the same hair color, you might vary this with hair length, or types, etc.

Next you are going to focus on more specific things and have people recognize how they are like others in a more personal way. Have them cluster themselves by month of birth, birth order, place of birth, or other possibilities. Allow talking for the last group and allow a reasonable amount of time for positive interaction. While these activities are going on, you need to be observing (maybe with the student list or seating chart in hand) so you can make some notes for yourself.

Now, let me introduce you to . . .

Student Interviews

Though time consuming, it will provide information you may rely upon all semester or year. This is a very powerful activity to use the first or second day of class. This is the way this goes.

1. You pair students who are not very familiar with each other. Try to prevent good friends from getting together. Sometimes this is impossible. Do the best you can. The object is for the class to know about this person. What they share should be positive, hopefully interesting, relevant, informative, etc. It is important to stress this is to be fun and informative, but absolutely not embarrassing or negative. Be ready to head off any digression here. I have not had it happen often, but you must make sure and protect each and every student, always.
2. Each pair will interview one another. Each student will have 5 minutes to interview their partner.

3. They must find out two to three interesting things that the student wants shared with the class. For example, they may want people to know they just finished some accomplishment like skiing, horseback riding, trip to Disney World, or a mission trip. They may not want everyone to know their boyfriend just dumped them, so require positive information.

4. This is the format: Student A (who is to mention the name of the person being introduced at least three times) says: I want to introduce Susie. Susie just moved here from Alaska. In Alaska Susie liked to ski and ice skate. One time Susie even saw a grizzly bear. Does anyone want to ask Susie a question? This is actually where students might get out of line with their questions. Limit response time. You may have to ask a question or two to get the ball rolling. Student B then introduces Student A and follows the same format.

You will find this may take all of the first and second day. However, you will learn your students' names and something about them that will make you remember them and be a better teacher for them than you can imagine. Using the information in a casual way, like, "Hey Susie, I would like to hear more about that grizzly bear one day." This will create a connection that is the beginning of trust. It works.

Sponge Activities

This is a very important consideration when your goal is to establish control and maintain control, all for the ultimate objective of teaching your students to become learners. You basically have the beginning of the day covered. You have planned and covered the material for days. Then one day you find yourself with more than 4 minutes before the class is to end.

Here are things you do *not* say:

- You may sit and talk quietly. Quietly is *not* going to happen ... ever.
- You may begin doing your homework. Ninety percent will not comply, they will talk.
- Sit quietly. Nope. Are you dreaming?

Instead, you reach for your index cards on your desk, where they are always handy, and engage the students in something relevant.

Example for Language Arts

1. First person to raise their hand and be able to write on the board the following words will receive two extra points on their next test (spelling, vocabulary, any discipline).
2. Take out a sheet of paper and write the last name of every American novelist you can remember. You have 4 minutes. At the end of 4 minutes, students swap papers and check every correct name on the paper, putting the number correct at the top. You go around the room and have students read the list on the paper they are grading. Instruct them not to repeat a name already read aloud.

THINK OF YOUR AREA OF INSTRUCTION, TAKING INTO CONSIDERATION THE AGE OF THE STUDENTS, AND CREATE SOME SPONGE ACTIVITIES.

From the Author

My philosophy of community service, specifically education, was passed down generation to generation. My grandmother told me I should be a teacher. I told her I was going to be an actress. I became both—all teachers are performers. Truthfully, I was born to teach. My great grandmother Lourraine Elliot Riddle (1870–1945) was raised in Tabernacle Community outside Lancaster, South Carolina, and went to Winthrop College at 16 years of age on a church scholarship, with the understanding she would teach in the local one-room schoolhouse. She returned and did teach, while helping her widowed mother raise the remaining four siblings along with five motherless cousins. She did not marry until she was 24 (an old maid), had one child, and kept on teaching. Later in Lancaster, she not only taught in the public school, but also at a night school for men working in the mill. At the time she was not even allowed to vote.

Well, you get the picture. When my youngest daughter called from college and asked how and when I realized women had gone so long without a voice, I had to pause. Pensively reflecting about the women in my life, I considered my Irish grandmother who got on a small ship with her sister in 1897 and sailed to a country that thought very little of the Irish (man or woman) to begin a life. I also thought about my southern grandmother, Lourraine's only child Ruth, who was raised to be sure she could do anything: hunt and fish with her father; sing, play piano and organ; graduate from Columbia College in 1917; and drive a car. Amazing that she was surprised when her three daughters all marched to a different drummer in the 1940s. One of them was my mother, who did not end up in education, but managed to find an Irish Catholic Yankee to marry. My grandmother never entirely adapted to that.

So when my daughter asked that question, I had to laugh. I was born with a voice. It has been with the encouragement of all the women of my life to participate in the most important field of education. I was told all my life that I could and should get into the community and participate, to contribute.

—**Sarah Ruth Clancy Ballard**

A good teacher is a doctor who heals ignorance, and an artist who inspires creativity.

—Author unknown

Author's Biography

Ballard received her BA in speech and drama from Converse College, an MEd in language arts from the University of Georgia, is teacher certified in language arts 7–12 and drama K–12, is a Georgia state one-act adjudicator, an International Thespian Society (ITS) troupe sponsor 1990–2000, and an ITS one-act adjudicator.

Born in South Carolina, Ballard was raised in Atlanta, Boston, and Philadelphia. After completing her degree from Converse College in Spartanburg, South Carolina, she married and moved with her husband to Atlanta, Georgia. While raising their three children, she worked in a variety of educational venues including Norcross First Methodist Kindergarten (director/teacher). She implemented the then new concept of Open Classroom, melded with an adaptation of Montessori methods. Several years later, she and a partner opened the Duluth Christian Academy of the Arts where instructors were hired to provide an assortment of art instruction including creative dramatics, painting, stained glass, ceramics, and modeling.

Later, returning to the role of student, she completed a master's of education, which allowed her to pursue her desire to teach high school in her community. The next 20 years were spent in secondary education teaching not only language arts, but also theater. During that time, she sponsored the inception of a literary magazine, still an annual publication at South Forsyth High School. She developed a theater program at that same school, which continues to flourish today.

Retirement brought her time to reflect upon her lifetime in education. Her last year caused her a good deal of consternation regarding behavior in the classroom today. Upon retirement, she decided to create a manual to assist the classroom teacher. Thus came *Control Is NOT a Four-Letter Word.*

CPSIA information can be obtained
at www.ICGtesting.com
Printed in the USA
LVOW07*2125080917
548023LV00005B/7/P

9 781681 239279